The South

ALABAMA ★ FLORIDA ★ MISSISSIPPI

By
Thomas G. Aylesworth
Virginia L. Aylesworth

CHELSEA HOUSE PUBLISHERS
New York   Philadelphia

Produced by James Charlton Associates
New York, New York.

First Printing

1   3   5   7   9   8   6   4   2

Library of Congress Cataloging-in-Publication Data

Aylesworth, Thomas G.
   The South: Alabama, Florida, Mississippi
Thomas G. Aylesworth, Virginia L. Aylesworth.
    p. cm. — (State reports)
   Includes bibliographical references and index.
   Summary: Discusses the geographical, historical, and cultural aspects of
Alabama, Florida, and Mississippi
   ISBN 0-7910-1044-9
      0-7910-1391-X (pbk.)
   1. Southern States—Juvenile literature. 2. Mississippi—Juvenile literature. 3. Alabama—Juvenile
literature. 4. Florida—Juvenile literature. [1. Southern States. 2. Mississippi. 3. Alabama. 4.
Florida.] I. Aylesworth, Virginia L. II. Title. III. Series: Aylesworth, Thomas G. State reports.

F209.3.A95   1991   90-28836
976—dc20   CIP
                                                   AC

Contents

Alabama

The great seal of Alabama was adopted in 1939; it is the same design that was used from 1819 until 1868. It is circular and bears a map of the state, showing its boundaries and rivers. Over the map is the word *Alabama,* and under it is inscribed "Great Seal."

State Flag

The Alabama state flag, officially designated in 1895, has a white background on which is a red cross of St. Andrew, which was the principal feature of the Confederate battle flag.

State Motto

Audemus Jura Nostra Defendere

The motto, which is Latin for "We Dare Defend Our Rights," was adopted in 1923.

Dogtrot cabins, so called because of the open breezeway running through the center of the house, dot rural Alabama. The breezeways provide relief from the summer heat.

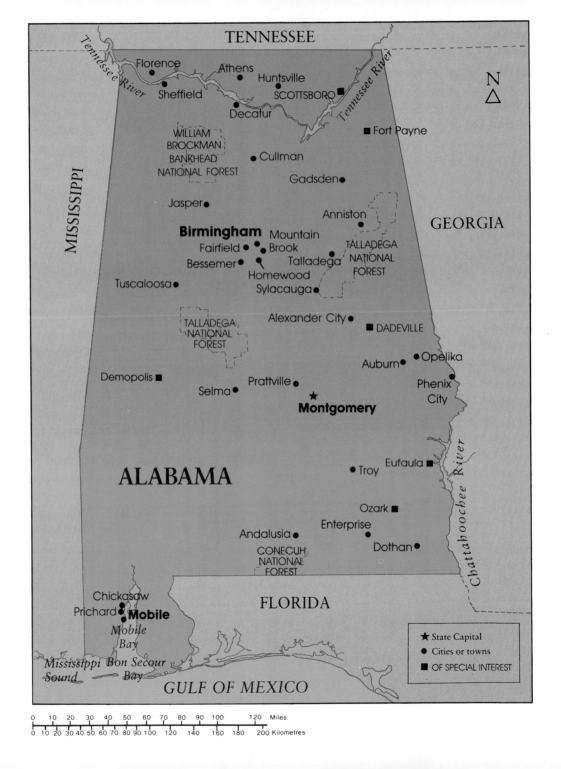

TENNESSEE

Tennessee River

Florence
Athens
Huntsville
Sheffield
SCOTTSBORO
Decatur
Tennessee River

Fort Payne

WILLIAM
BROCKMAN
BANKHEAD
NATIONAL FOREST

Cullman

Gadsden

MISSISSIPPI

Jasper

Anniston

GEORGIA

Birmingham   Mountain
Fairfield   Brook
Bessemer   Talladega   TALLADEGA
NATIONAL
FOREST
Homewood
Sylacauga

Tuscaloosa

TALLADEGA
NATIONAL
FOREST

Alexander City
DADEVILLE

Demopolis

Auburn   Opelika

Selma   Prattville
Phenix
City

★
Montgomery

ALABAMA

Troy   Eufaula

Ozark

Enterprise

Chattahoochee River

Andalusia
Dothan

CONECUH
NATIONAL
FOREST

Chickasaw
Prichard   Mobile

FLORIDA

Mobile
Bay

Mississippi   Bon Secour
Sound   Bay

GULF OF MEXICO

N
△

★ State Capital
● Cities or towns
■ OF SPECIAL INTEREST

0 10 20 30 40 50 60 70 80 90 100   120 Miles

0 10 20 30 40 50 60 70 80 90 100   120   140   160   180   200 Kilometres

State Capital

The first capital of Alabama was St. Stephens (1817-19). The towns of Huntsville (1819-20), Cahaba (1820-26), and Tuscaloosa (1826-46) also served as capitals. Finally, Montgomery was named the capital in 1846. The first capitol building was financed by city bonds in the amount of $75,000; a Greek Revival building, it was completed in 1847 but was destroyed in 1849. In 1850, the state legislature appropriated $60,000 to build a new building on the foundation of the old one. The present capitol building is also in the Greek Revival style, with Corinthian columns and a towering white dome. This building also served as the first Confederate capitol, and Jefferson Davis was sworn in as president here. Brick wings were added in 1885, 1905-1906, and 1911.

The state capitol building in Montgomery.

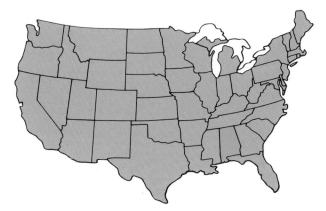

State Name and Nicknames

When Spanish explorers arrived in what was to become Alabama, the first Indians they met were the Alabama Indians, so the Europeans called the wide river there the Alabama

The yellowhammer, pine tree, and Camellia—the Alabama state bird, tree, and flower.

River. The territory later took its name from the river. The origin of the name of the Indian tribe is probably Choctaw—*Alba Amo,* meaning "thicket clearers" or "vegetation gatherers."

Alabama has no official nickname, but it is often called the *Yellowhammer State,* after the state bird. Because of the space center in Huntsville, it is also called *The Pioneer Space Capital of the World.* Other nicknames are *Heart of Dixie* and *Cotton State.*

State Flower

In 1927 the goldenrod, *Solidago juncea,* was named the state flower of Alabama. But in 1959, the law designating the goldenrod was repealed and the camellia, *Thea japonica,* was chosen to be the new state flower.

State Tree

In 1949, the southern pine, *Pinus palustris,* was adopted as the state tree. It is also called the longleaf yellow pine, the pitch pine, the hard pine, the heart pine, the turpentine pine, the rosemary pine, the brown pine, the fat pine, the longstraw pine, and the longleaf pitch pine.

State Bird

The yellowhammer, *Colaptes auratus,* was named the state bird in 1927. During the Civil War, Alabama soldiers were called *"yellowhammers"* because of the color of the uniforms of the Huntsville company, which were trimmed in bright yellow. This bird is also called the yellow-shafted flicker.

State Game Bird

In 1980, the wild turkey, *Meleagris gallopavo,* was designated the state game bird of Alabama.

State Dance

Named in 1981, the square dance is the official state dance.

State Fossil

Basilosaurus cetoides, an aquatic dinosaur about 55 feet long, was named the state fossil in 1984.

State Freshwater Fish

In 1975, the largemouth bass, *Micropterus punctulatus,* was designated as the state freshwater fish.

State Horse

The racking horse was named state horse in 1975.

State Mineral

Hematite, an iron ore, has been the state mineral since 1967.

State Nut

The pecan was named state nut in 1982.

State Rock

Marble was designated the state rock in 1969.

State Saltwater Fish

Named in 1955, the tarpon, *Tarpon atlanticus,* is the state saltwater fish.

The tarpon is Alabama's state saltwater fish.

State Song

"Alabama," with words by Julia S. Tutwiler and music by Edna Goeckel Gussen, was adopted as the state song in 1931.

Population

The population of Alabama in 1990 was 4,062,068, making it the 22nd most populous state. There are 78.6 persons per square mile—60 percent of the population live in towns and cities. Almost all Alabamians were born in the United States.

Geography and Climate

Bounded on the north by Tennessee, on the east by Georgia, on the south by Florida and the Gulf of Mexico, and on the west by Mississippi, Alabama has an area of 51,705 square miles, making it the 29th largest state. The climate is hot in the summer and mild in the winter, and there is abundant rainfall.

The highest point in the state is Cheaha Mountain in Cleburne County, at 2,407 feet, and the lowest point is at sea level along the Gulf of Mexico. In the south are coastal plains, and to the north lies a prairie known as the Black Belt because of the richness of the soil. Hills and the broken terrain of the Appalachian Mountains are found in the upper half of the state. The major waterways of the state are the Mobile, Alabama, Tombigbee, Coosa, Tallapoosa, Black Warrior,

Chattahoochee, and Tennessee rivers. The largest lake, Lake Guntersville, is man-made.

Industries

The principal industries of Alabama are pulp and paper, chemicals, electronics, apparel, textiles, primary metals, lumber and wood, food processing, fabricated metals, and automotive tires. The chief products are electronics, cast-iron and plastic pipe, fabricated steel products, ships, paper products, chemicals, steel, mobile homes, fabrics, and poultry products.

Agriculture

The chief crops of the state are peanuts, cotton, soybeans, hay, corn, wheat, potatoes, pecans, sweet potatoes, and cottonseed. Alabama is also a livestock state; there are estimated to be some 1.8 million cattle, 345,000 hogs and pigs, and 16.3 million chickens on its farms. Pine and hardwoods are harvested, and cement, clay, lime, sand, gravel, and stone are important mineral resources. Commercial fishing brings in some $33.8 million a year.

Government

The governor of Alabama is elected to a four-year term, as are the lieutenant governor, secretary of state, attorney general, auditor, treasurer, commissioner of agriculture and industries, and eight members of the state board of education. The state legislature, which meets annually, consists of a senate of 35 members and a house of representatives of 105 members. The state is divided into 35 senatorial districts, and each elects one senator. The state's 67 counties elect from 1 to 17 representatives, depending on their populations. The most recent

Sunset on Lake Guntersville. The largest artificial lake in Alabama, it covers 110 square miles and was formed by a dam on the Tennessee River.

state constitution was adopted in 1901. In addition to its two U.S. senators, Alabama has seven representatives in the U.S. House of Representatives. The state has nine votes in the electoral college.

History

More than 8,000 years ago, Mississippian Indians inhabited what was to be Alabama. When the Europeans arrived, they found Cherokee, Creek, Choctaw, and Chickasaw Indians living there.

It is possible that Alonso Álvarez de Piñeda, a Spaniard, sailed into Mobile Bay in 1519. In 1528, another Spaniard, Pánfilo de Narváez, sailed along the Alabama coast. The first man to explore the interior was also a Spaniard, Hernando de Soto, who entered Alabama from the northeast in 1540. Tristán de Luna, a Spaniard from Mexico, looked for gold in the area in 1559, and he set up a small settlement on

A reenactment of the Battle of Selma. Selma served as a Confederate supply post until it fell to Union troops on April 2, 1865.

Mobile Bay at the site of present-day Claiborne. He returned with his men to Mexico in 1561.

The French entered the territory in 1699. In 1702, two French-Canadian brothers, Pierre Le Moyne, Sieur d'Iberville, and Jean Baptiste Le Moyne, Sieur de Bienville, founded Fort Louis on the Mobile River. In 1711, floods forced them to move the settlement south to the spot

where Mobile is today. This became the first permanent European settlement in Alabama.

After the French and Indian War, England was given the French claim in Alabama. The Mobile Bay region became part of West Florida, and northern Alabama was part of the Illinois country.

Spain joined the Americans in the Revolutionary War in 1779, and in 1780, Mobile was

Dr. Martin Luther King, Jr., led a four-day civil rights march from Selma to Montgomery in March of 1965.

captured from the British by Bernardo de Gálvez. After the war, in 1783, England gave the Mobile area to Spain, but the rest of Alabama became a part of the United States. Then, in 1813, during the War of 1812, the United States took the Mobile area from Spain. In 1817, Alabama became a territory, with St. Stephens as its capital. In 1819, Alabama became the 22nd state in the Union.

When Alabama seceded from the Union in 1861, it named itself the Republic of Alabama. In that same year, Montgomery was named the capital of the Confederate States of America. (Even today, Montgomery is often referred to as the Cradle of the Confederacy.) However, the Confederate capital was soon moved to Richmond, Virginia. In 1864, the most important action of the Civil War in Alabama was fought—the Battle of Mobile Bay, in which the Union forces were triumphant. During the war, there were several Union raids in the state. After the war, Alabama was readmitted to the Union in 1868.

During the 1870s, prosperity began to return to the state. Railroads were built, and the iron and steel industry boomed, as did the lumber and textile industries. During World War I, shipbuilding became an important industry in Mobile, and great quantities of cotton and food were grown for the war effort.

During the Great Depression of the 1930s, some 60 Alabama banks failed, farmers lost their farms, and workers lost their jobs.

During World War II, Alabama had an increase in agricultural and industrial production. Thousands of soldiers were trained at Fort

McClellan, Fort Rucker, and Maxwell Air Force Base.

In the late 1940s, many scientists worked at the Redstone Arsenal in Huntsville to turn out the Jupiter, Redstone, and Saturn rockets, and the Apollo, Gemini, Mercury, and Pioneer satellites.

Civil rights problems arose in the 1950s, as Dr. Martin Luther King, Jr., led protests in Montgomery in 1955 and 1956. In 1956, Autherine Lucy became the first black to enroll in a previously all-white school in Alabama. Then, in 1963, Governor George Wallace twice blocked the admission of blacks to the University of Alabama; but President John F. Kennedy sent in the Alabama National Guard both times to stop this. In a five-day march from Selma to Montgomery in 1965, some 30,000 civil rights demonstrators gathered at the state capitol.

Sports

Many sporting events on the college and secondary school levels are held all over the state. In 1953, Birmingham won the Little League World Series. Although collegiate basketball is growing in popularity, college football is king in the state. The University of Alabama and Auburn University are perennial national powers, and both schools have appeared in numerous post-season bowl games.

Major Cities

Birmingham (population 284,413). Founded in 1870 and named after the English city, by 1900 Birmingham was being called "The Pittsburgh of the South" because of its steel mills. Today, the city is modern and progressive; it could be

The Birmingham Zoo is one of the largest in the southeast and is home to some very rare animals, including a white rhinoceros.

termed the heart of the "New South." It is a city of manufacturing, education, and culture.

Places to visit in Birmingham: the Statue of Vulcan, Arlington (1850), the Birmingham Museum of Art,

The 800 acres of Bellingrath Gardens were once home to local industrialist Walter D. Bellingrath, who bought the land in 1917 as a hunting preserve.

the Alabama Sports Hall of Fame Museum, Discovery Place, Sloss Furnaces National Historic Landmark, the Birmingham Zoo, the Birmingham Botanical Gardens, the Japanese Gardens, the Red Mountain Museum, the Ruffner Mountain Nature Center, and Rickwood Caverns State Park.

Mobile (population 200,452). Founded in 1711, Mobile is Alabama's only port city. It is a city full of Southern grace and Southern enterprise, and Mobile has managed to preserved its heritage in four historical districts: Church Street, DeTonti Square, Oakleigh Garden, and Old Dauphinway, where strollers are shaded on the oak-lined streets.

Places to visit in Mobile: Oakleigh (1830s), Bellingrath Gardens and Home, Richards-DAR House, the Fine Arts Museum of the South, the Exploreum Museum of Discovery, the Cathedral of the Immaculate Conception (1835), the Phoenix Fire Museum, the Carlen House Museum, Fort Conde Mobile Visitor Welcome Center, the Conde-

Charlotte Museum House (1824-1825), the Museum of the City of Mobile (1872), the Heustis Medical Museum, the Alabama State Docks, the Battleship USS Alabama Memorial Park, and the Malbis Greek Orthodox Church (1965).

Montgomery (population 177,857). Settled in 1814, this capital city was a great cotton market before the Civil War. Today, the city retains its pride in its history. It was from Montgomery that a telegram was sent ("Fire on Fort Sumter"), starting the Civil War. It was here that the Confederacy was born. And it was here that "Dixie" was set to music by Dan Emmett. Montgomery is a bustling city that retains its Southern charm.

Places to visit in Montgomery: the State Capitol (1851), the First White House of the Confederacy (1835), the Alabama Department of Archives and History, the Governor's Mansion, the Teague House (1848), the Rice-Semple-Haardt House (1855), the Lurleen B. Wallace Museum, the Murphy House

The Montgomery Museum of Fine Arts houses an impressive collection of works by southern artists, as well as an interactive gallery and studio for children.

(1851), the Old North Hull Street District, the Lower Commerce Street Historic District, the Montgomery Museum of Fine Arts, St. John's Episcopal Church (1855), the Dexter Avenue King Memorial Baptist Church (1877), the Montgomery Zoo, the Gayle Space Transit Planetarium, the Jasmine Hill Gardens, Hank Williams' Grave, Maxwell Air Force Base, and Fort Toulouse/Jackson Park National Historic Landmark.

Places to Visit

The National Park Service maintains eight areas in the state of Alabama: part of the Natchez Trace Parkway, Horseshoe Bend National Military Park, Russell Cave National Monument, Tuskegee Institute National Historic Site, Bankhead National Forest, Conecuh National Forest, Talladega National Forest, and Tuskegee National Forest. In addition, there are 22 state recreational areas.

Anniston: Dr. J. C. Francies Medical Museum and Apothecary. Built in 1850, this is a former doctor's office.

Clanton: Confederate Memorial Park. This Confederate cemetery also contains a museum of Civil War momentos.

Cullman: Ave Maria Grotto. Some 150 miniaturized replicas of famous churches and shrines are located on four acres of landscaped hillside.

Dauphin Island: Fort Gaines. Built in the 1850s, this Civil War fort contains a museum.

Decatur: Old Decatur and Albany Historic Districts. This neighborhood contains three pre-Civil War and 194 Victorian buildings.

Demopolis: Bluff Hall. Built in 1832, this is a restored Greek Revival mansion.

Dothan: Opera House. This 590-seat theater was built in 1915.

Eufaula: Seth Lore and Irwinton Historic District. There are 582 registered landmark buildings in this district.

Florence: W. C. Handy Home and Museum. This is the restored birthplace of the man who wrote "St. Louis Blues."

Fort Payne: Sequoyah Caverns and Campgrounds. Surrounding this fascinating cave are fields where deer and buffalo live.

Huntsville: The Space and Rocket Center. Exhibits of capsules and space shuttle objects, films, and tours of NASA activities.

Ozark: Holman Mansion. Built in 1912, this Greek Revival home has beautiful stained glass and handpainted stenciling on the walls.

Phenix City: Old Russell County Courthouse. This, the third-oldest courthouse in the state, was built in 1868.

Russellville: Dismals. This wilderness area contains trees more than 100 feet high,

The dramatic lighting in Sequoyah Caverns create the appearance of an underground palace.

natural bridges, and waterfalls.

Selma: Old Town Historic District. This district contains some 600 old buildings.

Talladega: International Motorsports Hall of Fame. The hall contains memorabilia and displays of motor sports.

Troy: Pike Pioneer Museum. Reconstructed buildings recreate nineteenth-century life here.

Tuscaloosa: Strickland House. Built in 1820, this is the oldest wooden house in the county.

Tuscumbia: Ivy Green. Built in 1820, this was the birthplace and early home of Helen Keller.

Tuskegee: George Washington Carver Museum. This includes exhibits and the original laboratory of the scientific genius.

Events

There are many events and organizations that schedule activities of various kinds in the state of Alabama. Here are some of them:

Sports: Alabama Deep-Sea Fishing Rodeo (Dauphin Island); Racking Horse World Celebration (Decatur); Wiregrass Quarter Horse Circuit Show (Dothan); International Billfishing Tournament (Gulf Shores); Senior Bowl Football Game (Mobile); greyhound racing at Mobile Greyhound Park (Mobile); Southern Livestock Exposition and Rodeo (Montgomery); stock and sports car races at the Alabama International Motor Speedway (Talladega); greyhound racing at Greenetrack (Tuscaloosa).

Arts and Crafts: Homespun (Athens); Dogwood Festival (Birmingham); Festival of the Arts (Birmingham); Southern Wildlife Festival (Decatur); Azalea Dogwood Festival (Dothan); Mentone Crafts Festival in Brow City Park (Fort Payne); Folklife Festival (Huntsville); Azalea Trail Festival (Mobile).

Music: Musical Explosion (Athens); Tennessee Valley Old Time Fiddlers Convention (Athens); Alabama Symphony Orchestra (Birmingham);

Decatur Chamber Orchestra (Decatur); W. C. Handy Music Festival (Florence); June Jam (Fort Payne); Huntsville Symphony (Huntsville); Panoply of the Arts Festival (Huntsville); Country Jam (Ozark); Cahawba Day (Selma).

Entertainment: Mayfest (Atmore); Homecoming and Powwow (Atmore); State Fair (Birmingham); Alabama Jubilee (Decatur); Spirit of America Festival (Decatur); Joe Wheeler Civil War Reenactment (Decatur); Christmas on the River (Demopolis); Alabama Air Fair (Dothan); National Peanut Festival (Dothan); Indian Summer Days (Eufaula); DeKalb County VFW Agricultural Fair (Fort Payne); Mardi Gras Celebration (Gulf Shores); Sea Oats Jazz and Arts Festival (Gulf Shores); National Shrimp Festival (Gulf Shores); Northeast Alabama State Fair (Huntsville); Mardi Gras (Mobile); Blessing of the Shrimp Fleet (Mobile); Greater Gulf State Fair (Mobile); Jubilee (Montgomery); South Alabama Fair (Montgomery);

The W. C. Handy Festival in Florence features the Street Strut and walking parade, as well as planned and impromptu musical performances.

Russell County Courthouse Fair (Phenix City); Central Alabama Fair (Selma); Tale Telling Festival (Selma); Helen Keller Festival (Sheffield).

Tours: Christmas Heritage Tour (Bessemer); Plantation Homes Tour (Birmingham); Christmas in Canebrake (Demopolis); Eufaula Pilgrimage (Eufaula); Heritage Tour (Florence); Cotton Harvest (Huntsville); Historic Mobile Tours (Mobile); Black Heritage Tour (Selma); Historic Selma Pilgrimage (Selma); Tuscaloosa Heritage Week (Tuscaloosa).

Hank Aaron holds the major-league record for the most career home runs (755) and runs batted in (2,297); he played 23 seasons in the majors.

Theater: Princess Theater (Decatur); Alabama Shakespeare Festival (Montgomery); "The Miracle Worker" (Tuscumbia).

Famous People

Many famous people were born in the state of Alabama. Here are a few:

Hank Aaron b. 1934, Mobile. Hall of Fame baseball player

Mel Allen b. 1913, Birmingham. Baseball announcer

Tallulah Bankhead 1903-1968, Huntsville. Award-winning stage and film actress

Hugo Black 1886-1971, Harlan. Supreme Court justice

Lyman Bostock 1950-1978, Birmingham. Baseball player

Nat "King" Cole 1917-1965, Montgomery. Pop singer

Angela Davis b. 1944, Birmingham. Black militant

John Drew b. 1954,

Tallulah Bankhead was well known for her intelligence, beauty, and exuberance. To many she symbolized the best of the "roaring twenties."

Vredenburgh. Basketball player

Louise Fletcher b. 1936, Birmingham. Academy Award-winning actress: *One Flew Over the Cuckoo's Nest*

George Foster b. 1948, Tuscaloosa. Baseball player

Kenneth Gibson b. 1932, Enterprise. First black

mayor of Newark, New Jersey

William C. Gorgas 1854-1920, near Mobile. Physician and conqueror of malaria and yellow fever

Lionel Hampton b. 1913, Birmingham. Jazz vibraphonist

W. C. Handy 1873-1958, Florence. Blues composer

Bo Jackson b. 1962, Bessemer. Football and baseball player

Kate Jackson b. 1948, Birmingham. TV actress: *The Rookies, Charlie's Angels*

Helen Keller 1880-1968, Tuscumbia. Deaf and blind woman who became an example of achievement

Coretta Scott King b. 1927, Marion. Civil rights leader and widow of Dr. Martin Luther King, Jr.

Harper Lee b. 1926, Monroeville. Pulitzer Prize-winning novelist: *To Kill A Mockingbird*

Joe Louis 1914-1981, Lexington. Heavyweight boxing champion

Willie Mays b. 1931, Westfield. Hall of Fame baseball player

Willie McCovey b.1938, Mobile. Hall of Fame baseball player

Jim Nabors b. 1933, Sylacauga. TV actor and singer: *The Andy Griffith Show; Gomer Pyle, U.S.M.C.*

Jesse Owens 1913-1980,

Helen Keller's extraordinary life was dramatized in William Gibson's award-winning play and film The Miracle Worker.

Danville. Olympic gold-medal winner in track and field

Satchel Paige 1906-1982, Mobile. Hall of Fame baseball pitcher

Claude Pepper 1900-1989, Dudleyville. Senator, congressman, and champion of the aged

Walker Percy b. 1916, Birmingham. Novelist: *The Last Gentleman, Love in the Ruins*

Wilson Pickett b. 1941, Prattville. Rhythm-and blues-singer

Holland "Howlin' Mad" Smith 1882-1967, Seale. World War II Marine Corps general

Pine Top Smith 1904-1929, Troy. Boogie-woogie pianist

Ken Stabler b. 1945, Foley. Football quarterback

Bart Starr b. 1934, Montgomery. Hall of Fame football quarterback

Don Sutton b. 1945, Clio. Baseball pitcher

Toni Tenille b. 1943, Montgomery. Pop-rock singer of The Captain and Tenille

John H. Vincent 1832-1920, Tuscaloosa. Methodist bishop and founder of the Chautauqua movement

Dinah Washington 1924-1963, Tuscaloosa. Blues singer

Hank Williams 1923-1953, Georgiana. Country-and-western singer

Tammy Wynette b. 1942, Red Bay. Country-and-western singer

Early Wynn b. 1920, Hartford. Hall of Fame baseball pitcher

Colleges and Universities
There are many colleges and universities in Alabama. Here are the more prominent, with their locations, dates of founding, and enrollments.

Alabama Agricultural and Mechanical University, Normal, 1873, 4,500.

Alabama State University, Montgomery, 1874, 4,456.

Auburn University, Auburn, 1856, 21,701.

Birmingham-Southern College, Birmingham, 1856, 1,931.

Huntingdon College, Montgomery, 1854, 838.

Jacksonville State University, Jacksonville, 1883, 8,620.

Livingston University, Livingston, 1840, 1,761.

Oakwood College, Huntsville, 1896, 1,223.

Samford University, Birmingham, 1841, 4,159.

Spring Hill College, Mobile, 1830, 938.

Troy State University, Troy, 1887, 3,589.

Tuskegee Institute, Tuskegee, 1881, 3,510.

University of Alabama, at *Tuscaloosa,* 1831, 19,432; at *Birmingham,* 1969, 15,508, in *Huntsville,* 1950, 8,082.

Where to Get More Information
Alabama Bureau of Tourism and Travel
532 South Perry Street
Montgomery, Alabama 36104
Or call 1-800-252-2262

Florida

The state seal of Florida, adopted in 1868 and revised in 1985, is circular. As mandated by the state legislature, the design elements of the seal are the sun, a sabal palmetto tree, a steamboat, and a female Indian. Around the circle is written "Great Seal of the State of Florida" and "In God We Trust."

State Flag

The state flag of Florida has a white background with two diagonal red stripes, representing the bars on the Confederate flag. In the center is the state seal. The flag was adopted in 1899.

A sweeping look at Miami Beach. Miami Beach is in fact an island connected to the city of Miami by bridges and causeways.

★ State Capital
● Cities or towns
■ OF SPECIAL INTEREST

The state capitol building in Tallahassee was completed in 1977; on display there is the original Florida state constitution.

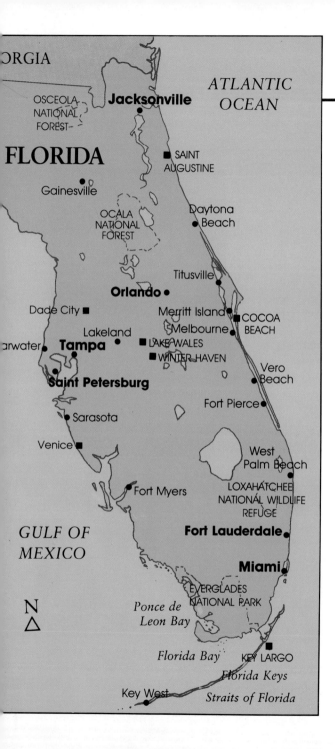

State Capital

Tallahassee has been the capital of Florida since 1824. In 1826, a two-story masonry building was constructed to be the capitol building. In 1845, the entire building was torn down and a new brick building was built. A copper dome and four wings were added in 1902. By 1972, the building was deemed to be inadequate, and the legislature authorized a capitol complex with legislative chambers and offices and a 307-foot, 22-story executive office building. Dedicated in 1978, it cost $43,070,741.

State Name and Nicknames

Florida was discovered on Easter Sunday in 1513 by the Spanish explorer Ponce de León. He therefore named it for the Spanish Easter Feast of Flowers—Pascua Florida.

Florida is most often called the *Sunshine State,* but it is also referred to as the *Alligator State,* the *Everglades State,* and the *Southernmost State.* Because of the importance of the citrus industry, it is sometimes called the *Orange State.*

State Flower

In 1909, the orange blossom,

The orange blossom is the state flower.

from the tree of the family *Rutaceae,* was named the state flower.

State Tree

Sabal palmetto, the sabal palmetto palm, was adopted as the state tree in 1953. It is also called the cabbage palm, the cabbage palmetto, the palmetto, the tree palmetto, and Bank's palmetto.

State Bird

The mockingbird, *Mimus polyglottos,* named state bird in 1927, was the winner of a statewide vote.

State Air Fair

The Central Florida Air Fair was adopted as the state air fair in 1976.

State Animal

The Florida panther, *Felis concolor,* was selected as state animal in 1982.

State Beverage

In 1967, orange juice from the species *Citrus sinensis* and

The mockingbird is the state bird.

its hybrids was chosen as the state beverage.

State Festival

Named in 1980 as state festival was "Calle Ocho — Open House 8," a festival held annually in Dade County.

State Freshwater Fish

The Florida largemouth bass, *Micropterus salmoides floridanus,* was adopted as state freshwater fish in 1975.

State Gem

The moonstone, chosen in 1970, is the state gem.

State Litter Control Symbol

The litter control trademark of the Florida Federation of Garden Clubs, Inc., "Glenn Glitter," was adopted in 1978.

State Marine Mammal

In 1975, the manatee, *Trichechus latirostris*, also called the sea cow, was named the state marine mammal in 1975.

State Pageant

"Indian River," presented annually in Brevard County, was adopted as state pageant in 1979.

State Play

The historical pageant "Cross and Sword," presented annually in St. Augustine, was chosen as state play in 1973.

State Saltwater Fish

The Atlantic sailfish, *Istiophorus platypterus*, was designated as state saltwater fish in 1975.

State Saltwater Mammal

The porpoise, *Delphinus delphis,* was named the state saltwater mammal in 1975.

State Shell

The shell of *Pleuroploca gigantea,* the horse conch or giant band shell, was adopted as state shell in 1969.

State Stone

Agatized coral was named the state stone in 1979.

State Song

In 1935, Stephen Foster's "Old Folks at Home," also known as "Swanee River," was named the state song.

Population

The population of Florida in 1990 was 13,003,362, making it the fourth most populous state. There are 240.1 persons per square mile—84.3 percent of the population live in towns and cities. About 89 percent of all Floridians were

The Calle Ocho festival, held in Little Havana, celebrates the region's Cuban heritage.

born in the United States. The largest groups of people born in foreign countries have come from Cuba, Canada, England, Germany, and Russia.

Visitors feed the alligators at Homosassa Springs in central western Florida. Tourism is important to the local economy here, as it is throughout the state.

Geography and Climate

Bounded on the north by Georgia and Alabama, on the east by the Atlantic Ocean, on the south by the Atlantic Ocean and the Gulf of Mexico, and on the west by the Gulf of Mexico and Alabama, Florida has an area of 54,153 square miles, making it the 22nd largest state. The climate is tropical in the south and subtropical in the north. The highest point in the state, at 345 feet, is near Lakewood, and the lowest is at sea level along the Atlantic and the Gulf.

Florida is flat, with a few rolling hills. The major waterways in the state are the St. Johns, St. Marys, Perdido, Apalachicola, and Suwannee. Lake Okeechobee is the state's largest lake.

Industries

The principal industries of the state of Florida are services, trade, manufacturing, and tourism. The chief manufactured products are electric and electronic equipment, transportation equipment, food, printing and publishing, and machinery.

Agriculture

The chief crops of the state are citrus fruits, vegetables, potatoes, melons, strawberries, and sugar cane. Florida is also a livestock state. There are estimated to be some 1.97 million cattle, 150,000 hogs and pigs, 7,360 sheep, and 13.5 million chickens on its farms. Pine, cypress, and cedar are harvested, and cement, phosphate rock, and crushed stone are important mineral resources. Commercial fishing brings in some $185.9 million a year.

Government

The governor of Florida serves a four-year term, as do the attorney general, the commissioner of agriculture, the comptroller, the secretary of state, the commissioner of education, and the treasurer. The state legislature, which meets annually, consists of a 40-member senate and a 120-member house of representatives. Senators serve four-year terms, and representatives serve two-year terms. All legislators are elected by district. The most recent state constitution was adopted in 1968. In addition to its two U.S. senators, Florida has 19 representatives in the U.S. House of Representatives. The state has 21 votes in the electoral college.

History

Before the Europeans arrived, what was to become Florida was inhabited by the Calusa Indians in the south, the Timucua in the central and northeast regions, and the Apalachicola in the northwest. The Calusa were hunters and fishermen, while the Timucua and Apalachicola were farmers and hunters.

The Spanish explorer Juan Ponce de León had heard rumors of a fountain of youth

Juan Ponce de León landed near what is now St. Augustine on April 2, 1513; he named the area Pascua Florida because it was discovered during the Feast of Flowers.

in what is now Florida. He arrived in 1513 and claimed the area for Spain, naming it Florida. He returned to Florida in 1521 to start a colony, but he died after a battle with the Indians, and his followers left the region.

Seminole Indians fought U.S. Marines in the swamps of the Everglades during the Second Seminole War, 1835-1842.

Hernando de Soto, landed in the Tampa Bay area in 1539. From there he led his men to the Mississippi River. In 1564, some French Huguenots established a colony on the St. Johns River near what is now Jacksonville; there they built Fort Caroline. When King Philip II of Spain heard about the colony, he sent an expedition to drive them from Spanish territory. In 1565, these Spaniards massacred the French and founded St. Augustine.

By the mid-1700s, England had established colonies to the north of Florida, and France had colonies to the west. When wars broke out between the English and the French, Spain sided with France. Then, in 1762, England captured Havana, Cuba, and in 1763, Spain traded Florida for Havana.

The British divided Florida up into the East Florida and West Florida colonies. West Florida then included parts of what are now Alabama, Mississippi, and Louisiana. In

Another Spaniard, Pánfilo de Narváez, brought 400 men to the southwest coast of Florida and traveled north in search of gold. But he and most of his men were killed in shipwrecks.

Still another Spaniard,

This photo, taken in 1861, shows the Louisville Blues of the 1st Alabama Regiment encamped near Pensacola.

War (1816-1821), Jackson captured Fort St. Marks on the Gulf of Mexico, marched east to the Suwannee River, and defeated some of the Seminole Indians. In 1821, Spain finally agreed to turn over Florida to the United States.

Florida became part of the United States in 1821 and was named the Territory of Florida in 1822. Finally, Florida was admitted to the Union as a slave state in 1845 —the 27th state in the Union.

In 1861, Florida seceded from the Union and later joined the Confederacy. Early in the Civil War, Union forces captured most of the coastal towns in Florida, but in 1865, a small band of Confederate troops successfully defended Tallahassee from the Union army. Florida was readmitted to the Union in 1868.

During the 1880s, Florida began to boom. Phosphate deposits were discovered, and many swamps were drained. New land was opened for development, and

1779, the Spaniards returned to West Florida. The British, weakened by the Revolutionary War, surrendered West Florida to Spain in 1781, and Spain took over the rest of Florida in 1783.

In the early 1800s, Florida was the only part of the southeast that did not belong to the United States. The Florida settlers fought the Spanish, but Spain still refused to sell the region to the United States. A group of settlers rebelled in 1812 and declared their independence, but they were stopped. During the War of 1812, Spain permitted England to use Pensacola as a naval base. American General Andrew Jackson invaded Florida and captured Pensacola.

During the First Seminole

citrus groves were planted. Resort cities blossomed. In the early 1900s, more swamps were drained, and the land was opened to more agriculture.

Then the land boom began, with its reports of fantastic profits to be made from land in Florida. The bubble burst in 1926, forcing many banks to close. Hurricanes struck the Atlantic coast in 1926 and 1928. Before the state could recover, the Great Depression of the 1930s took place.

The state began to recover economically during World War II. The location of Florida was vital to the defense of the country, and several air and naval bases were established in the state. After the war, manufacturing continued to grow. New industries sprouted up, and in the 1950s, Cape Canaveral became a major space and rocket center. Florida today is thriving, and new residents continue to arrive there.

Al Lang Stadium in St. Petersburg is the current spring training home of the St. Louis Cardinals.

Sports

Many sporting events on the collegiate and secondary school levels are played all over the state. Florida State University, the University of Florida, and the University of Miami are perennial football powers. All three schools have appeared in numerous post-season bowl games. On the professional level, the Miami Dolphins of the National Football League play in Joe Robbie Stadium, and the Tampa Bay Buccaneers play in Tampa Stadium. The Miami Heat and the Orlando Magic of the National Basketball Association play in Florida. Eighteen major league baseball teams have their spring training camps in Florida and play exhibition games in the early spring. The Basque sport of Jai Alai is also popular, and there are several frontons along the east coast of the state.

Major Cities

Jacksonville (population 540,920). Settled by the British in 1822, it was first known as Cowford. But when Florida became part of the United States, the town was renamed to honor Andrew Jackson. After the Seminole Wars, the city became a prosperous harbor town. During the Civil War, Jacksonville was occupied four times by the Union troops. After the war, it became a popular winter resort. Today, it is a city of skyscrapers and a major business center.

Places to visit in Jacksonville: the Jacksonville Zoological Park, the Cummer Gallery of Art, the Museum of Science and History, the Jacksonville Art Museum, the Kingsley Plantation State Historic Site, and Little Talbot Island State Park.

Miami (population 346,865). Settled in 1870, Miami was only a remote tropical village until 1896, when the East Coast Railway arrived. In the 1920s, the land boom brought 25,000 real estate salesmen to town. Today, it is home to more than 3,400 manufacturing companies, 170 banks, 636 hotels and motels, 4,509 restaurants, 6,556 churches and synagogues, and 36 hospitals.

Places to visit in Miami: the Vizcaya Museum and Gardens, the Museum of Science and Space Transit Planetarium, the Historical Museum of South Florida, the Cloisters of the Monastery of St. Bernard de Clairvaux, the Japanese Garden, the Metrozoo, the Parrot Jungle and Gardens, Seaquarium, the Planet Ocean, the Gold Coast Railroad, the Monkey Jungle, the Bayside Marketplace, Little Havana, Lummus Park, the Miccosukee Indian Village, and the Wilderness Experiences/Everglades Institute.

A dramatic view of the Jacksonville skyline. The city is Florida's largest in geographical area, having incorporated most of the surrounding county.

St. Petersburg (population 238,647). Founded in 1876, the fourth most populous city in the state is a favorite with vacationers and retirees. It is also a center of the aerospace and appliance industries.

Places to visit in St. Petersburg: the St. Petersburg Historical Museum, the Hass Museum, the Salvador Dali Museum, the Museum of Fine Arts, the Science Center of Pinellas Country, Great Explorations, the Planetarium, Florida's Sunken Gardens, and The Pier.

Tallahassee (population 81,548). Founded in 1824, the capital city retains both the grace of the old plantation days and its rustic pioneer past. It is also a center of lumber and wood production, printing, publishing, and food production.

The Villa Vizcaya, now a museum, was built between 1914 and 1922 by James Deering, an heir to the International Harvester fortune. It cost an astonishing 15 million dollars.

The style known as Miami Art Deco was developed in the late 1930s on the south end of Miami Beach. More than 800 of these buildings have been preserved in Art Deco Historic District.

Places to visit in Tallahassee: the Historic Old Capitol-State Building, the State Capitol, the Governor's Mansion (1957), the First Presbyterian Church (1832), the Tallahassee Junior Museum, the LeMoyne Art Foundation, The Columns (1830), the Museum of Florida History, the Alfred B. Maclay State Gardens, the and the San Marcos de Apalache State Museum.

Tampa (population 271,523). Settled in 1823, it traces its history back to Fort Brooke, which was built to oversee the Seminole Indians. During the Civil War, it was the subject of raids and began to decline as a business center. It grew again with the building of the South Florida Railroad. Tampa was a major staging area in the Spanish-American War. Today, it is a major port and the business hub of the west coast of Florida.

Places to visit in Tampa: Ybor City, the Ybor City State Museum, Busch Gardens—"The Dark Continent," the Tampa Museum of Art, the Hillsborough County Historical Commission Museum, the Museum of Science and Industry, Adventure Island, Lowry Park, and the Waterfront.

Places to Visit

The National Park Service maintains 12 areas in the state of Florida: Castillo de San Marcos National Monument, Fort Jefferson National

A scenic look at the sunrise over Tallahassee. The city was the only Confederate capital east of the Mississippi that was not captured by Union troops during the Civil War.

Monument, Fort Matanzas National Monument, De Soto National Memorial, Fort Caroline National Memorial, Biscayne National Park, Everglades National Park, part of the Gulf Islands National Seashore, Cape Canaveral National Seashore, Apalachicola National Forest, Ocala National Forest, and Osceola National Forest. In addition, there are 59 state recreation areas.

Bradenton: Manatee Village Historical Park. The renovated buildings open for exhibit include the Stephens House, an excellent example of a rural Florida farmhouse.

Brooksville: Weeki Wachee Spring. An underwater ballet, comedy, tableaus, and acrobatics can be seen in the extraordinary underground auditorium.

Clearwater: Clearwater Marine Science Center and

Sea Aquarium. The center, which rescues marine mammals and sea turtles, includes an aquarium, research laboratories, and educational programs.

Clermont: House of Presidents. Life-size wax

A shuttle launching at the Kennedy Space Center; it was from here that the U.S. launched its first satellite in 1958. The center draws more than 1.5 million visitors a year.

figures of the United States Presidents are displayed in period settings.

Coral Gables: Fairchild Tropical Garden. The gardens spread over 83 acres containing 5,000 varieties of tropical plants.

Dade City: Pioneer Florida Museum. Ten acres of old buildings contain thousands of artifacts, as well as an old train depot and engine.

Fort Lauderdale: Ocean World. Performing dolphins and sea lions are featured in the shows presented here.

Fort Myers: Edison Winter Home and Botanical Gardens. The House and guesthouse where Thomas A. Edison spent almost 50 winters are open to the public.

Gainesville: Marjorie Kinnan Rawlings State Historical Site. This farmhouse contains memorabilia of the author of *The Yearling.*

Hollywood: Six Flags—Atlantis. This 65-acre amusement park, with over

80 attractions, includes many water rides.

Homosassa Springs: Doll Museum. More than 1,700 antique and modern dolls are displayed here.

Kennedy Space Center: Spaceport USA. Here are films, displays, and tours of the facilities, including the Air Force Station and Museum, as well as the Missile Exhibit.

Key West: Ernest Hemingway Home and Museum. Built in 1851, this is the house where the author often wrote.

Kissimmee: Walt Disney World, Epcot Center, and MGM Studios. This world-famous complex is the chief attraction in Florida.

Lake Wales: The Bok Tower Gardens. The Bok Singing Tower, 205-feet high, provides bell music throughout the day.

Marineland: Marineland of Florida. Hundreds of fish of all sizes are on exhibit.

Miami Beach: Art Deco District. Some 800 buildings

The amazing performances of the dolphins and other aquatic creatures make Marineland a popular tourist attraction.

of early twentieth-century design can be seen in an area of one square mile.

Orlando: Sea World of Florida. The marine park features a huge aquarium and a killer whale show.

Palm Beach: Henry Morrison Flagler Museum. Built in 1901, the 55-room home of the railroad builder contains period furnishings and special collections.

Pensacola: Naval Air Station. The Naval Aviation Museum displays more than 100 full-size aircraft.

Perry: Cracker Homestead. Here is a homestead of double-notched squared logs and outbuildings from the early days of Florida.

St. Augustine: Spanish Quarter. The restoration of the colonial village of the 1700s includes several houses and a blacksmith shop.

Sarasota: Sarasota Jungle Gardens. The area contains more than 5,200 varieties of tropical plants and many tropical birds.

Tarpon Springs: Dodecanese Boulevard. Shrimp boats and sponge boats painted with Greek designs are anchored along this waterfront street.

Venice: Circus Winter Quarters. Here are a rehearsal hall and an arena in which are held occasional performances by the Ringling Bros. and Barnum and Bailey circus.

West Palm Beach: Lion Country Safari, Inc. One can drive a car through this 640-acre park, which contains more than 1,000 wild animals.

Winter Haven: Cypress Gardens. The great botanical gardens contain exotic plants and a theme park with varied areas.

Winter Park: The Charles Hosmer Morse Museum of American Art. There are fine examples of Tiffany glass in the large collection .

The Orange Bowl in Miami. The first Orange Bowl game, won by the University of Miami, was played in 1933.

Events

There are many events and organizations that schedule activities of various kinds in the state of Florida. Here are some of them.

Sports: Greyhound racing at Sanford-Orlando Kennel Club (Altamonte Springs); All-Florida Championship Rodeo (Arcadia); High Goal Polo (Boca Raton); greyhound racing at Naples-Fort Myers Greyhound Track (Bonita Springs); National Surfing Tourneys (Cocoa Beach); Junior Orange Bowl Festival (Coral Gables); auto races at Daytona International Speedway (Daytona Beach); greyhound racing at Daytona Beach Kennel Club (Daytona Beach); De Land-St. Johns River Festival (De Land); Deep-Sea Fishing Rodeo (Destin); Amateur Invitational Golf Tournament (Fernandina Beach); horse racing at Gulfstream Park (Fort Lauderdale); Southwest Florida Championship Rodeo (Fort Myers); horse racing at Hialeah Park (Hialeah); greyhound racing at Hollywood Greyhound Track (Hollywood); Rodeo and Frontier Days (Homestead); Sportfishing Festival (Islamorada); greyhound racing at Jacksonville Kennel Club (Jacksonville); Tournament Players Championship (Jacksonville Beach); Lipton International Players Championship (Key Biscayne); Silver Spurs Rodeo (Kissimmee); Key Colony Beach Sailfish Tournament (Marathon); Governor's Cup Rowing Regatta (Melbourne); Sun Dek Surfing Classic (Melbourne); Sebastian Offshore Sportfishing Tournament (Melbourne); greyhound racing at Flagler Dog Track (Miami); greyhound racing at Biscayne Dog Track (Miami); horse racing at Calder Race Course (Miami); Orange Bowl Game (Miami); Grand Prix of Miami (Miami); International Boat Show (Miami); Doral/Ryder Open PGA Golf Tournament (Miami); Miami/Budweiser Unlimited Hydroplace Regatta (Miami); Lee Evans Bowling Tournament (Miami); South Florida Auto Show (Miami); Speckled Perch Festival (Okeechobee); Cattleman's Rodeo (Okeechobee); Florida Citrus Sports Holiday (Orlando); harness racing at Ben White Raceway (Orlando); Antique Car

Meet (Ormond Beach); Palatka Horseman's Rodeo (Palatka); Captain Billfish Tournament (Panama City); Open Spearfishing Tournament (Panama City); Treasure Ship/Roy Martin King Mackerel Tournament (Panama City); greyhound racing at Ebro Greyhound Track (Panama City); Deep Sea Fishing Rodeo (Panama City Beach); Billfish Tournament (Pensacola); stock car racing at Five Flags Speedway (Pensacola); Pompano Beach Fishing Rodeo (Pompano Beach); harness racing at Pompano Park Raceway (Pompano Beach); auto racing at Sunshine Speedway (St. Petersburg); Southern Ocean Racing (St. Petersburg); greyhound racing at St. Petersburg Kennel Club (St. Petersburg); sailboat regattas (St. Petersburg); Sarasota Classic (Sarasota); Sarasota Sailing Squadron Labor Day Regatta (Sarasota); International Tarpon Tournament (Sarasota); Sebring 12-hour Endurance Race (Sebring); Hall of Fame Bowl (Tampa); greyhound racing at Tampa Track (Tampa); Walt Disney World Golf Classic (Lake Buena Vista); polo at Gulfstream Polo Field (West Palm Beach); greyhound racing at Palm Beach Kennel Club (West Palm Beach).

Arts and Crafts: Boynton's GALA (Boynton Beach); Space Coast Art Festival (Cocoa Beach); Riverside Art Festival (Jacksonville); Coconut Grove Arts Festival (Miami); Art Deco Weekends (Miami Beach); Festival of the Arts (Miami Beach); Naples Shell Show (Naples); Images and Arts Fiesta (New Smyrna Beach); Azalea Festival (Palatka); Spring Festival of the Arts (Panama City); Great Gulfcoast Arts Festival (Pensacola); Sanibel Shell Fair (Sanibel Island).

Music: Florida Symphonic Pops (Boca Raton); Florida Atlantic Theater (Boca Raton); the Florida Orchestra (Clearwater); Old Time Music Championship (Dade City); Philharmonic of Florida (Fort Lauderdale); Civic Music Concerts (Fort Lauderdale); Hollywood Festival of the Arts (Hollywood); Jazz Festival (Hollywood); Greater Hollywood Philharmonic Orchestra (Hollywood); Jacksonville Symphony (Jacksonville); Delius Festival (Jacksonville); Florida National

A violinist with the New World Symphony, this country's first and only full-time training orchestra.

Jazz Festival (Jacksonville); Bluegrass Festival (Kissimmee); Miami City Ballet (Miami); Greater Miami Opera Association (Miami); Orlando Opera Company (Orlando); Florida Symphony Orchestra (Orlando); Promenade Concerts (Palm Beach); Palm Beach Opera (Palm Beach); the Florida Orchestra (St. Petersburg); Florida Tournament of Bands (St. Petersburg); Sarasota Jazz Festival (Sarasota); Sarasota Opera Company (Sarasota); Music Festival of Florida (Sarasota); Concert Series (Sarasota); Summer Swamp Stomp (Tallahassee); Florida Orchestra (Tampa); Florida Folk Festival (White Springs); Jeanie Audition's and Ball (White Springs); Bach Festival (Winter Park).

Entertainment: Florida Seafood Festival (Apalachicola); De Soto County Fair and Livestock Exposition (Arcadia); Black Gold Jubilee Celebration (Belle Glade); Boca Festival Days (Boca Raton); Hernando County Fair (Brooksville); Seafood Festival (Cedar Key); Watermelon Festival (Chiefland); Fun 'n Sun Festival (Clearwater); Pasco County Fair (Dade City); Pioneer Florida Festival (Dade City); Cracker Day (Deerfield Beach); Chautauqua Festival Day (De Runiak Springs); Manatee

Festival (De Land); Central Florida Balloon Classic (De Land); Volusia County Fair and Youth Show (De Land); Turn-of-the-Century Holiday (De Land); Bon Festival (Delray Beach); Seafood Festival (Destin); Highland Games and Scottish Festival (Dunedin); Isle of Eight Flags Shrimp Festival (Fernandina Beach); Southwest Florida Fair (Fort Myers); Pageant of Light (Fort Myers); Shrimp Festival (Fort Myers Beach); St. Lucie County Fair (Fort Pierce); Seafood Festival

(Fort Walton Beach); Billy Bowlegs Festival (Fort Walton Beach); Animal Day (Gainesville); Heritage Fair (Gainesville); Museum Open House (Gainesville); Florida Derby Festival (Hallandale); Seminole Indian Tribal Fair (Hallandale); Hollywood Sun 'n Fun Festival (Hollywood); Broward County Fair (Hollywood); Indian Key Festival (Islamorada); Gator Bowl Festival (Jacksonville); Beaches Festival Weekend Celebration (Jacksonville Beach);

Located in one of Miami's oldest neighborhoods, the Coconut Grove Playhouse was built in 1926 and held its first theatrical season in 1956. Most of its productions are premiers.

Leif Erikson Day Pageant (Jensen Beach); Turtle Watch (Jensen Beach); Official Florida State Air Fair (Kissimmee); Boating Jamboree (Kissimmee); Battle of Olustee Reenactment (Lake City); North Florida Air Show (Lake City); Columbia County Fair (Lake City); Sun and Fun EAA Fly-in (Lakeland); Grant Seafood Festival (Melbourne); Turtle Crawl (Melbourne); Orange Bowl Festival (Miami); Carnival Miami/ Calle Ocho Festival (Miami); Italian Renaissance Festival (Miami); International Festival (Miami); Miccosukee Indian Arts Festival (Miami); Collier County Agricultural Fair (Naples); Chasco Fiesta (New Port Richey); Southeastern Youth Fair (Ocala); Orlando Scottish Highland Games (Orlando); Central Florida Fair (Orlando); Pioneer Days Folk Festival (Orlando); Putnam County Fair (Palatka); Flagler Anniversary Open House (Palm Beach); Bay County Fair (Panama City); Indian Summer Seafood Festival (Panama City Beach); Mardi Gras (Pensacola); Fiesta of the Five Flags (Pensacola); Creek Indian Pow-Wow (Pensacola); Blue Angel Air Show (Pensacola); Florida Forest Festival (Perry);

Seafood Festival (Pompano Beach); Boat Parade (Pompano Beach); Blessing of the Fishing Fleet (St. Augustine); Spanish Night Watch (St. Augustine); Greek Landing Day Festival (St. Augustine); Days in Spain (St. Augustine); Maritime Festival (St. Augustine); British Night Watch (St. Augustine); Holiday Regatta of Lights (St. Augustine); International Folk Fair (St. Petersburg); Renaissance Festival (St. Petersburg); Festival of States (St. Petersburg); Medieval Fair (Sarasota); Bradford County Fair (Starke); Martin County Fair (Stuart); Battle Reenactment (Tallahassee); Flying High Circus (Tallahassee); Springtime Tallahassee (Tallahassee); Spring Farm Days (Tallahassee); North Florida Fair (Tallahassee); December on the Farm (Tallahassee); Florida State Fair (Tampa); Gasparilla Pirate Invasion (Tampa); Festival of Epiphany (Tarpon Springs); Valiant Air Command Air Show (Titusville); Venetian Sun Fiesta (Venice); South Florida Fair and Exposition (West Palm Beach); Sunfest (West Palm Beach); Florida Citrus Festival and Polk County Fair (Winter Haven).

Tours: Historic Home Tour (Jacksonville); Old Island Days (Key West); Garden Club Tour of Homes (St. Augustine).

Theater: Caldwell Playhouse (Boca Raton); Florida Shakespeare Festival (Coral Gables); Parker Playhouse (Fort Lauderdale); Passion Play (Lake Wales); Coconut Grove Playhouse (Miami); Jackie Gleason Theater of the Performing Arts (Miami Beach); Royal Poinciana Playhouse (Palm Beach); "Cross and Sword" (St. Augustine); The Players of Sarasota (Sarasota); Asolo Performing Arts Center (Sarasota).

Participants in the Turtle Watch on Jensen Beach have the rare opportunity to observe the giant turtles nesting in the sand.

Famous People

Many famous people were born in the state of Florida. Here are a few:

Julian "Cannonball" Adderley 1928-1975, Tampa. Jazz saxophonist

Elizabeth Ashley b.1941, Ocala. Stage and film actress: *Ship of Fools, Coma*

Pat Boone b.1934, Jacksonville. Pop singer

Don Carter b.1930, Miami. Championship bowler

Jacqueline Cochran 1910-1980, Pensacola. First woman flyer to exceed the speed of sound

Faye Dunaway b.1941, Bascom. Academy Award-winning actress: *Network*

Chris Evert b.1954, Fort Lauderdale. Champion tennis player

Steve Garvey b.1948, Tampa. Baseball player

Artis Gilmore b.1949, Chipley. Basketball player

Bobby Goldsboro b.1942, Marianna. Country-and-western singer

Dwight Gooden b. 1964, Tampa. Baseball pitcher

Deacon Jones b.1938, Eatonville. Football player

Edmund Kirby-Smith 1824-1893, St. Augustine. Last Confederate commander to surrender

Butterfly McQueen b.1911, Tampa. Film actress: *Gone With The Wind, The Mosquito Coast*

At her death, Jacqueline Cochran held more speed, altitude, and distance records than any other pilot, male or female.

After the fall of the Confederacy, Edmund Kirby-Smith became president of the University of Nashville and later taught mathematics at the University of the South.

Charles E. Merrill 1885-1956, Green Cove Springs. Broker and co-founder of Merrill Lynch brokerage

Patrick O'Neal b.1927, Ocala. Film and television actor: *The Way We Were, The Stepford Wives*

Charles H. Percy b. 1919, Pensacola. U.S. Senator

Sidney Poitier b.1927, Miami.

Academy Award-winning actor: *Lilies of the Field, Guess Who's Coming to Dinner*

A. Philip Randolph 1889-1979, Crescent City. Civil rights leader

Esther Rolle b.1933, Pompano Beach. Television actress: *Maude, Good Times*

Charles E. Merrill was also one of the founders of Family Circle *magazine, which began publication in 1932.*

Joseph "Vinegar Joe" Stilwell 1883-1946, Palatka. World War II general

Ben Vereen b.1946, Miami. Dancer and actor: *Roots, Tenspeed and Brown Shoe*

Jack Youngblood b.1950, Monticello. Football player

Colleges and Universities

There are many colleges and universities in Florida. Here are the more prominent, with their locations, dates of founding, and enrollments.

Barry College, Miami Shores, 1940, 5,900.

Bethune-Cookman College, Daytona Beach, 1872, 2,145.

College of Boca Raton, Boca Raton, 1963, 1,150.

Flagler College, St. Augustine, 1963, 1,159.

Florida Agricultural and Mechanical University, Tallahassee, 1887, 7,469.

Florida Atlantic University, Boca Raton, 1964, 11,481.

Florida Institute of Technology,

A. Philip Randolph published the Messenger, *a radical black magazine, and was instrumental in ending segregation in defense plants and the military.*

Melbourne, 1958, 4,117.

Florida International University, Miami, 1965, 19,529.

Florida Southern College, Lakeland, 1885, 1,955.

Florida State University, Tallahassee, 1857, 28,000.

Jacksonville University, Jacksonville, 1934, 2,445.

Rollins College, Winter Park, 1885, 2,070.

St. Thomas University, Miami, 1961, 2,500.

Stetson University, De Land, 1883, 3,090.

University of Florida, Gainesville, 1853, 34,022.

University of Miami, Coral Gables, 1925, 13,790.

University of North Florida, Jacksonville, 1965, 7,727.

University of South Florida, Tampa, 1956, 31,638.

University of Tampa, Tampa, 1931, 2,476.

University of West Florida, Pensacola, 1967, 7,576.

Where to Get More Information

Florida Division of Tourism
Visitor Inquiry
126 Van Buren Street
Tallahassee, Florida 32301

Sunset at the University of Tampa.

Mississippi

The great seal of the state of Mississippi was adopted in 1817. It is circular and bears the figure of an eagle holding an olive branch (representing peace) in its right talon and three arrows (representing war) in its left. Around the circle is inscribed "The Great Seal of the State of Mississippi."

State Flag

The state flag of Mississippi, adopted in 1894, shows the state's ties both to the United States and the Confederacy. In the upper left corner, with a red background, are two diagonal lines of blue with 13 stars on them—a representation of the Confederate battle flag. The rest of the flag carries wide stripes of red, white, and blue—the colors of the flag of the United States.

State Motto

Virtute et Armis

The Latin motto means "by valor and arms" and was suggested in 1894.

Dunlieth is a National Historic Landmark and is one of more than 500 antebellum homes in Natchez.

★ State Capital
● Cities or towns
■ OF SPECIAL INTEREST

TENNESSEE

Mississippi River

ARKANSAS

LOUISIANA

MISSISSIPPI

ALABAMA

Mississippi River

LOUISIANA

GULF OF MEXICO

N
△

Corinth
Holly Springs
HOLLY SPRINGS NATIONAL FOREST
New Albany
Oxford
Tupelo
Clarksdale
HOLLY SPRINGS NATIONAL FOREST
TOMBIGBEE NATIONAL FOREST
Amory
Aberdeen
Cleveland
Grenada
West Point
SCOTT
Indianola
Greenwood
Starkville
Columbus
Greenville
Leland
TOMBIGBEE NATIONAL FOREST
Kosciusko
Louisville
DELTA NATIONAL FOREST
Yazoo City
Philadelphia
Canton
Vicksburg
BIENVILLE NATIONAL FOREST
Pearl
Meridian
Jackson
Natchez
Brookhaven
Laurel
DE SOTO NATIONAL FOREST
HOMOCHITTO NATIONAL FOREST
Hattiesburg
Columbia
McComb
DE SOTO NATIONAL FOREST
Picayune
Ocean Springs
Moss Point
Bay Saint Louis
Biloxi
Pascagoula
Gulfport
SHIP ISLAND

0 10 20   40   60   80   100   120   140   160   180   Miles
0 10 20   40   60   80   100   120 140   160 180 200   250   300 Kilometres

State Capital

The first capital of Mississippi was Natchez (1798-1802), followed by Washington (1802-1817), Natchez again (1817-1821), and Columbia (1821-1822). Finally, in 1822, Jackson was selected as the permanent capital. The first capitol building in Jackson was completed in 1839. In 1903, the present building was dedicated. The outside of this beaux arts structure is made of Bedford limestone and Georgia granite. Blue Vermont marble, Italian white marble, Belgian black marble, and black New York marble are found on the inside. The dome rises to a height of 180 feet, and is surmounted by an eight-foot eagle coated with gold leaf. The capitol building cost $1,093,641.

Though dedicated in 1903, the state capitol building in Jackson is still referred to as the New Capitol.

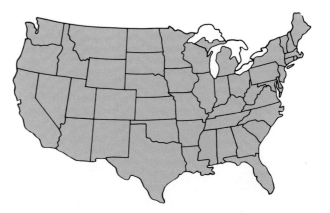

State Name and Nicknames

The state of Mississippi was named after the Mississippi River, which had several other names. Gulf Coast Indians called the river the Malbouchia, while the Spanish discoverers called it Rio del Espíritu Santo and Rio Grande de Florida. Later, the French named it the Colbert and the St. Louis River. Indians in the northwest called it the Mississippi, a Chippewa Indian word meaning "Large River"; that name appears on LaSalle's map of 1695.

The most common nickname for Mississippi is the *Magnolia State* because there are so many of those trees in the state. But it is also known as the *Eagle State* and the *Border-Eagle State* since there is an eagle on the state seal. There are so many bayous in the state that it has been named the *Bayou State*. And because of the multitude of catfish in its streams and swamps Mississippi is called the *Mud-Cat State*.

The magnolia flower.

State Flower

In 1900, the children of Mississippi voted the flower of the magnolia tree, *Magnolia grandiflora*, the state flower. However, the state legislature did not adopt it officially until 1952.

State Tree

Magnolia grandiflora, the magnolia, was named the state tree in 1938. It is also called the evergreen magnolia.

State Bird

The mockingbird, *Mimus polyglottos*, was selected as the state bird of Mississippi in 1944.

State Waterfowl

Aix sponsa, the wood duck, was named the state waterfowl in 1974.

State Beverage

Milk was selected as the state beverage in 1984.

State Fish

In 1974, the largemouth bass, *Micropterus salmoides*, was adopted as the state fish.

State Fossil

The prehistoric whale was named the state fossil in 1981.

The Mississippi state bird.

State Insect

Adopted in 1980, the honey bee, *Apis mellifera,* is the state insect.

State Land Mammal

The white-tailed deer, *Odocoileus virginianus,* was selected as the Mississippi land mammal in 1974.

State Shell

In 1974, the oyster shell was named the state shell.

State Water Mammal

The bottlenosed dolphin, *Tursiops truncatus,* was selected as state water mammal in 1974.

State Song

The state song, selected in 1962, is "Go, Mississippi," written by Houston Davis.

Population

The population of Mississippi in 1990 was 2,586,443, making it the 31st most populous state. There are 54.2 persons per square mile—47.3 percent of the population live in towns and cities. Almost all Mississippians were born in the United States.

Geography and Climate

Bounded on the north by Tennessee, on the east by Alabama, on the south by the Gulf of Mexico and Louisiana, and on the west by Louisiana and Arkansas, Mississippi has an area of 47,689 square miles, making it the 32nd largest state. The climate is semitropical. The highest point in the state, at 806 feet, is Woodall Mountain in Tishomingo County, and the lowest point is at sea level along the Gulf of Mexico.

In the northeast are high sandy hills and a prairie belt of rich black soil. In the north-central section are wooded ridges. In the south are low, fertile river deltas, with some bluffs, sandy terraces, and piney woods. The Major waterways in Mississippi are the Mississippi, Big Black, Yazoo, Goldwater,

The "Mighty Mississippi" still provides a passage for riverboat cruises, much as it did a hundred years ago.

Sunflower, Tallahatchie, Pearl, Pascagoula, Tombigbee, and Tennessee rivers. Many of the lakes, including Barnetts Reservoir, Sardis Reservoir, and Arkabutla Reservoir, are man-made.

Industries

The principal industries of the state of Mississippi are food processing, seafood, trade, and agriculture. The chief manufactured products are apparel, lumber and wood products, food products, electrical machinery and equipment, and transportation equipment.

Agriculture

The chief crops of the state are cotton, soybeans, and rice. Mississippi is also a livestock state. There are estimated to be 1.4 million cattle, 180,000 hogs and pigs, 4,500 sheep, and 387 million chickens on its farms. Pine, oak, and hardwoods are harvested. Sand, gravel, clay, and crushed stone are important mineral resources. Commercial fishing brings in some $44 million each year.

Government

The governor of Mississippi is elected to a four-year term, as are the lieutenant governor, the secretary of state, the treasurer, the state auditor of public accounts, the superintendent of education, the attorney general, and the commissioners of agriculture and commerce, insurance, and land. The state legislature, which meets annually, consists of a 52-member senate and a 122-member house of representatives. They are elected to four-year terms. The most recent state constitution was adopted in 1890. In addition to its two U.S. senators, Mississippi has five representatives in the U.S. House of Representatives. The state has seven votes in the electoral college.

History

Before the Europeans arrived, what was to become Mississippi was the home of three powerful Indian tribes. These were the Chickasaw, who lived in the north and west; the Choctaw in the southern part; and the Natchez in the southwest. These three dominant tribes ruled other tribes: the Chakchiuma, Tunica, and Yazoo along the Yazoo River, and the Biloxi and Pascagoula on the Gulf coast.

Hernando de Soto, the Spanish explorer, passed through the territory in 1540-1541. He was looking for gold but instead discovered the Mississippi River. In 1682, a Frenchman, Robert Cavelier, Sieur de la Salle, traveled down the Mississippi from the Great Lakes to the Gulf of Mexico, claiming the whole region for the French. He also named it Louisiana, for King Louis XIV of France. This claim included what is now Mississippi.

In 1699, Pierre Le Moyne,

A depiction of the charge of the 6th Missouri Regiment at the Battle of Vicksburg.

Sieur d'Iberville, a French explorer, established the first settlement, Old Biloxi, which is now Ocean Springs. In 1716, another French settlement was made by his brother Jean Baptiste Le Moyne, Sieur de Bienville. Called Fort Rosalie, it is now Natchez. In 1736, the British helped the Chickasaw defeat the French in the northern part of what is now Mississippi, and after the French and Indian War, the British were given the area. The southern part of Mississippi became part of the West Florida province, and almost all the rest joined the Georgia Colony.

During the Revolutionary War, loyalties were divided. But in 1781 the Spaniards invaded West Florida, and in 1783, it was ceded to the Spanish by the British. After the Revolution, northern Mississippi was given to the United States. In 1798, the Mississippi Territory was set up, and in 1812, West Florida was added to the region. The Mississippi Territory was divided into the state of Mississippi and the Alabama Territory when Mississippi was admitted to the Union as the 20th state in 1817.

In 1861, Mississippi became the second state to secede from the Union. More than 80,000 Mississippians served in the Confederate army, and important battles were fought at Corinth, Harrisburg (now Tupelo), Holly Springs, Iuka, Meridian, and Port Gibson. In 1864, the South won the Battle of Brice's Cross Roads. The most important military engagement in Mississippi was the Battle of Vicksburg, which ended when the city fell to General Ulysses S. Grant in 1863. In 1867, Mississippi was placed under Union military rule and was not readmitted to the Union until 1870.

In the early 1900s, Mississippi agriculture and

industry began to boom.
During World War I, Payne
Field and Camp Shelby
became major training
camps, and the lumber
industry prospered. During
the Great Depression of the
1930s, the state suffered, but
soon oil was discovered.
During World War II, many
war plants were set up in
Mississippi, and Pascagoula
became an important ship
assembly center.

After the war, the number
of industrial plants in the
state more than doubled.
Today, Mississippi is
growing industrially but still
manages to retain its
Southern charm.

Sports

Many sporting events on
the collegiate and secondary
school levels are scheduled
all over the state. The
University of Mississippi and
Mississippi State University
are perennial national football powers, and both schools
have appeared in numerous
post-season bowl games.

*All of this country's space shuttles
are tested at the John C. Stennis
Space Center in Hancock County.*

Major Cities

Biloxi (population 49,311).
Settled in 1699, this is the
oldest town in the Mississippi
Valley. It has been a popular
resort since the 1840s; even
today, although it is a leading
oyster and shrimp fishing
center, it is an exquisite city,
with magnolia trees,
camellias, azaleas, roses, and
crepe myrtle blooming along

the streets, and oaks draped
with Spanish moss.

> *Things to see in Biloxi:* Beauvoir-
> Jefferson Davis Shrine, the
> Biloxi Lighthouse (1848), the
> Old Biloxi Cemetery, the
> Tullis-Toledano Manor (1856),
> Deer Island, Keesler Air Force
> Base, Small Craft Harbor, and
> the Vieux Marche Walking
> Tour.

Jackson (population
202,895). Founded in 1821,
the capital city was built in
the center of the state. It was
laid out in a checkerboard
pattern at the suggestion of
Thomas Jefferson, and the
original plans called for the
reservation of every other
square as a park or green. In
1863 the city was reduced to
ashes by Union General
William T. Sherman, bringing
it the nickname
"Chimneyville." But it was
rebuilt, and today it is a city
of charm.

> *Things to see in Jackson:* the State
> Capitol (1903), the Governor's
> Mansion (1842), the State
> Historical Museum, the
> Confederate Monument
> (1891), the Archives and
> History Building, the Oaks
> (1846), the Manship House

(1857), the Museum of Natural Science, the Municipal Art Gallery, the Mississippi Museum of Art, the Mynelle Gardens, the Jackson Zoological Park, Battlefield Park, the Mississippi Agriculture and Forestry Museum and National Agricultural Aviation Museum, and the Mississippi Petrified Forest.

Meridian (population 46,577). Settled in 1831, Meridian is an industrial, agricultural, and retailing center.

Thing to see in Meridian: Merrehope (1858), the Frank W. Williams House (1886), the Meridian Museum of Art, the Jimmie Rodgers Museum, and the Naval Air Station.

Places to Visit

Clarksdale: Delta Blues Museum. Memorabilia, videotapes, and slide programs of blues music are displayed.

Columbus: Historic homes. There are more than 100 homes in Columbus that date to before the Civil War, and several are open to visitors.

Corinth: Curlee House.

Built in 1857, it served as headquarters for generals Bragg, Halleck, and Hood during the Civil War.

Greenville: River Road Queen. This is a replica of a nineteenth-century paddlewheel steamboat.

Greenwood: Florewood River Plantation. Crops are worked and harvested at this recreation of a plantation of the 1850s.

Grenada: Historic Old Grenada. This is a motor and walking tour of old homes

and churches.

Gulfport: National Space Technology Laboratories. This is the second-largest NASA field station in the United States.

Natchez: Historic Springfield Plantation. Believed to be the oldest mansion in Mississippi, the house, with its hand-carved woodwork, was built between 1786 and 1790.

Ocean Springs: Shearwater Pottery. A fine pottery, established in 1928, displays

An aerial view of Jackson, Mississippi.

Rowan Oak, William Faulkner's home, features a wall on which he wrote the outline to his Pulitzer Prize-winning novel The Fable.

glazedware created by the founder.

Oxford: Rowan Oak. Once the home of the novelist William Faulkner, the house contains original furnishings and memorabilia.

Pascagoula: Old Spanish Fort and Museum. Built by the French in 1718, it is the oldest fortified structure in the Mississippi Valley.

Port Gibson: First Presbyterian Church. Built in 1859, it contains chandeliers from the steamboat *Robert E. Lee.*

Tupelo: Elvis Presley Park and Birthplace. In a park stands the small frame house where the singer lived the first three years of his life.

Vicksburg: McRaven Home Civil War Tour. Heavily shelled during the Siege of Vicksburg in 1863, this home is an architectural record of Vicksburg history.

Woodville: Rosemont Plantation. Built around 1810, this was the home of Jefferson Davis and his family.

Yazoo City: Wister Gardens. Fourteen acres of azaleas, roses, tulips, crysanthemums, hyacinths, jonquils, crocuses, camellias, sasanquas, hollies, and other flowers are open to the public.

Events

There are many events and organizations that schedule activities of various kinds in the state of Mississippi. Here are some of them.

Sports: Mississippi Deep-Sea Fishing Rodeo (Gulfport); Mississippi State Horse Show (Jackson).

Arts and Crafts: Delta Jubilee (Clarksdale).

Music: Delta Blues Festival (Greenville); Jackson Symphony (Jackson); Lively Arts Festival (Meridian); Jimmie Rodgers Memorial Festival (Meridian).

Entertainment: Mardi Gras (Biloxi); Shrimp Festival (Biloxi); Seafood Festival (Biloxi); Deep South Festival (Columbus); Civil War Living History Expo (Holly Springs); Dixie National Livestock Show (Jackson); Mississippi State Fair (Jackson); Central Mississippi Fair and State Dairy Show (Kosciusko); Lighted Azalea Trail (Louisville); Southeast Mississippi State Fair (Meridian); Faulkner Conference (Oxford); Mardi Gras (Pascagoula); Landing of D'Iberville (Pascagoula); Flagship Festival (Pascagoula); Jackson County Air Show (Pascagoula); Jackson County Fair (Pascagoula); Mardi Gras (Pass Christian); Blessing of the Fleet (Pass Christian); Choctaw Indian Fair (Philadelphia); Neshoba County Fair (Philadelphia); Tobacco Spit in Billy John Crumpton's Pasture (Raleigh).

Tours: Garden Club Pilgrimage (Biloxi); Pilgrimage (Columbus); Spring Pilgrimage (Gulfport); Pilgrimage (Holly Springs); Pilgrimage (Natchez); Garden and Home Pilgrimage (Ocean

Each year, thousands of tourists visit this two-room house in Tupelo where Elvis Presley was born.

Springs); Garden Club Pilgrimage (Pascagoula); Garden Club Pilgrimage (Pass Christian); Spring Pilgrimage (Vicksburg).

Theater: Anniversary of the Landing of D'Iberville Pageant (Ocean Springs); "Gold in the Hills" (Vicksburg).

Famous People

Many famous people were born in the state of Mississippi. Here are a few:

Henry Armstrong 1912-1988, Columbus. Boxer who held featherweight, light-weight, and welterweight titles at the same time

Red Barber b.1908, Columbus. Sports broadcaster

Craig Claiborne b.1920, Sunflower. Gourmet and food writer

Bo Diddley b.1928, McComb. Rock-and-roll singer

Charles Evers b.1922, Decatur. Civil rights leader

Medgar Evers 1925-1963, Decatur. Civil rights leader

William Faulkner 1897-1962, New Albany. Nobel Prize-winning novelist: *The Sound and The Fury, Absalom, Absalom!*

Bobbie Gentry b.1944, Chickasaw County. Country-and-western singer

Fanny Lou Hamer 1917-1977, Montgomery County. Civil rights leader

Jim Henson 1936-1990, Greenville. Creator of the Muppets

William Faulkner's writing was deeply rooted in the American South, but his themes were universal, insuring his popularity here and abroad.

James Earl Jones b.1931, Tate County. Award-winning stage and screen actor: *The Great White Hope, Field of Dreams*

B. B. King b.1925, Itta Bena. Rhythm-and-blues singer

John Avery Lomax 1867-1948, Goodman. Folk musicologist

Jimmie Lunceford 1902-1947, Fulton. Jazz band leader

Archie Manning b.1949, Drew. Football quarterback

Archie Moore b.1916, Benoit. Light-heavyweight boxing champion

Willie Morris b.1934, Jackson. Novelist and nonfiction writer: *North Toward Home, The Last of the Southern Girls*

Dave Parker b.1951, Calhoun. Baseball player

Elvis Presley 1935-1977, Tupelo. Rock-and-roll singer

Leontyne Price b.1927, Laurel. Operatic soprano

Charles Pride b.1939, Sledge.

Early on, Eudora Welty prepared for a career in advertising, but the success of her first short stories enabled her to pursue her love of writing full-time.

Country-and-western singer

Stella Stevens b. 1936, Yazoo City. Movie actress: *The Courtship of Eddie's Father, The Poseidon Adventure*

William Grant Still 1895-1978, Woodville. Composer, conductor

Ike Turner b.1939, Clarksdale. Pop singer

Conway Twitty b.1933, Friar's Point. Country-and-western singer

Eudora Welty b.1909, Jackson. Pulitzer Prize-winning short-story writer and novelist: *The Optimist's Daughter*

Tennessee Williams 1911-1983, Columbus. Two-time Pulitzer Prize-winning dramatist: *A Streetcar Named Desire, Cat on a Hot Tin Roof*

Oprah Winfrey b.1954, Kosciusko. TV talk-show hostess

Richard Wright 1908-1960, near Natchez. Novelist: *Native Son, Black Boy*

Lester Young 1909-1959, Woodville. Jazz saxophonist

Colleges and Universities

There are many colleges and universities in Mississippi. Here are the more prominent, with their locations, dates of founding, and enrollments.

Alcorn State University, Lorman, 1871, 2,847.

Delta State University, Cleveland, 1924, 3,820.

Jackson State University, Jackson, 1877, 7,152.

Millsaps College, Jackson, 1890, 1,443.

Mississippi College, Clinton, 1826, 4,221.

Mississippi State University, Mississippi State, 1878, 13,141.

Mississippi University for Women, Columbus, 1884, 2,085.

Mississippi Valley State University, Itta Bena, 1946, 1,691.

University of Mississippi, University, 1844, 10,370.

University of Southern Mississippi, Hattiesburg, 1910, 11,544

William Carey College, Hattiesburg, 1911, 1,600.

How to Get More Information

Division of Tourism
Mississippi Department of Economic Development
P.O. Box 22825
Jackson, Mississippi 39205
Or call 1-800-647-2290

Bibliography

General

Aylesworth, Thomas G., and Virginia L. Aylesworth. *Let's Discover the States: The South*. New York: Chelsea House, 1988.

Alabama

Carpenter, Allan. *Alabama*. rev. ed. Chicago: Children's Press, 1978.

Fradin, Dennis B. *Alabama in Words and Pictures*. Chicago: Children's Press, 1980.

Gray, Daniel S. *Alabama: A People, A Point of View*. Dubuque, Iowa: Kendall/Hunt, 1977.

Griffith, Lucille B. *Alabama: A Documentary History*, rev. and enl. ed. University, Alabama: University of Alabama Press, 1972.

Hamilton, Virginia B. *Alabama: A Bicentennial History*. New York: Norton, 1977.

Hamilton, Virginia B. *Alabama, A History*. New York: Norton, 1984.

Walker, Alyce B. ed. *Alabama: A Guide to the Deep South*, rev. ed. New York: Hastings House, 1975.

Florida

Carpenter, Allan. *Florida*, rev. ed. Chicago: Children's Press, 1979.

Fradin, Dennis B. *Florida in Words and Pictures*. Chicago: Children's Press, 1980.

Jahoda, Gloria. Florida: *A Bicentennial History*. New York: Norton, 1976.

Jahoda, Gloria. Florida: *A History*. New York: Norton, 1984.

Patrick, Rembert W., and A. C. Morris. *Florida Under Five Flags*, 4th ed. Gainesville, Florida: University Presses of Florida, 1967.

Smith, Mary Ellen. *Florida*. New York: Coward, 1970.

Tebeau, Charlton W. A *History of Florida*, rev. ed. Miami, Florida: University of Miami Press, 1981.

Mississippi

Carpenter, Allan. *Mississippi*, rev. ed. Chicago: Children's Press, 1978.

Fraden, Dennis B. *Mississippi in Words and Pictures*. Chicago: Children's Press, 1980.

Lowry, Robert, and W. H. McCardle. *A History of Mississippi*. Spartanburg, South Carolina: Reprint Company, 1978.

McLemore, Richard A., ed. *A History of Mississippi*. 2 vols. Jackson, Mississippi: University Press of Mississippi, 1973.

Newton, Carolyn S., and P. H. Coggin. *Meet Mississippi*. Huntsville, Alabama: Strode, 1976.

Rowland, Dunbar. *History of Mississippi, the Heart of the South*. 2 vols. Spartanburg, South Carolina: Reprint Company, 1978.

Sansing, David G. *Mississippi: Its People and Culture*. Minneapolis: Denison, 1981.

Skates, John Ray. *Mississippi: A Bicentennial History*. New York: Norton, 1979.

Skates, John R. *Mississippi, A History*. New York: Norton, 1985.

Photo Credits/Acknowledgments

Photos on pages 3 (top) 5, 6-7, 9-13, 15-19 courtesy of the State of Alabama Bureau of Tourism & Travel; pages 14, 20 (top), 21 courtesy of the Alabama State Archives; page 20 (bottom) courtesy of the Atlanta Braves; pages 3 (middle), 23-25, 27, 28, 30, 34-40, 43 courtesy of the Florida Department of Commerce/Division of Tourism; pages 29, 41 and 42 courtesy of the Miami Convention & Visitors Bureau; pages 31-33 courtesy of the Florida State Archives; pages 44 and 45 (top) courtesy of the Florida Department of State/Division of Library & Information Services; pages 3 (bottom) and 47 courtesy of the Mississippi Department of Economics & Community Development; pages 48-49, 51, 53, 56, 57, 59, 61 courtesy of the Mississippi Office of Travel & Tourism; pages 55 and 60 courtesy of the State of Mississippi/Department of Archives & History; page 45 (bottom) courtesy of Merrill Lynch & Co., Inc.; page 58 courtesy of Robert Jordan

Cover photograph courtesy of the Alabama Bureau of Tourism & Travel